Youth Congregations and the Emerging Church

Graham Cray

Bishop of Maidstone

GROVE BOOKS LIMITED

RIDLEY HALL RD CAMBRIDGE CB3 9HU

Contents

The Cover Illustration is by Peter Ashton

Church Army and the Grove Evangelism Series

Church Army has over 350 evangelists working in five areas of focus, at the cutting edge of evangelism in the UK. It co-sponsors the publication of the Grove Evangelism Series as part of its aim of stimulating discussion about evangelism strategies, and sharing its experience of front-line evangelism.

Further details about Church Army are available from:
Church Army, Independents Road, Blackheath, London SE3 9LG.
Telephone: 020 8318 1226. Fax: 020 8318 5258.
Registered charity number: 226226

First Impression February 2002
ISSN 1367-0840
ISBN 1 85174 491 6

1
Introduction

'It is impossible to avoid ecclesiology in the communication of the gospel, for the gospel does not come as a pure message but issues from, and gives rise to, specific communities; and such communities will adopt certain characteristics which they believe express the gospel in churchly form.'

Timothy Yates[1]

This booklet addresses a number of interrelated issues: the urgent need to win young people to Christ and to disciple them within his church; the existence of a growing number of youth congregations, set up for this purpose; the emergence of a new, even novel, cultural context for mission and evangelism in the UK; and, above all, the need for a grounded and principled theology of the church which allows us to remain faithful to our Anglican heritage but respond flexibly and imaginatively to a changing world.

Changing Practice in Youth Ministry

Since the publication of the *English Church Census* in 1991,[2] youth ministry in the UK has undergone a substantial and relatively effective transformation,[3] and a number of core values have been identified.

It has been recognised that youth ministry must be relational. It involves the establishment of genuine relationships to ensure that the evangelism is not manipulative.

Young people are empowered to take responsibility for their own ministry rather than merely being provided with programmes where the ministry is done to or for them. The best evangelists among young people are young people. Youth cells *led by young people* have become an essential part of the strategy. Schools-based work has become increasingly important.

Good practice in youth mission is holistic. The old divisions between evangelism, social action, education and nurture are largely broken down. Young people are met at their point of need. It is simply assumed that part of their need is to come to faith in Christ. In areas of social deprivation it involves working towards long-term social transformation based on an incarnational commitment.[4]

Youth ministry now takes a 'process' rather than a 'crisis' approach. It assumes that, in an age of huge ignorance of the Christian faith belonging to the Christian community will probably precede believing the Christian message, which will precede any necessary changes in lifestyle. Youth Alpha has been an important tool in this respect. There is a serious attempt to enable young people to grow in discipleship and Christian lifestyle.

Youth ministry is understood to be incarnational. It involves entering young people's world(s) in order to plant the gospel and the church there. It does not necessarily intend to draw young people back into a church culture which is alien to them if that culture is dying. That is to say it is not a 'bridge' strategy but a genuine commitment to new forms of church for a new cultural era.

Worship, in particular appropriate music, is critical for any youth evangelism which is serious about integrating young people into the church. Taizé and 'alternative worship' play an important part, but far greater numbers respond to more obviously contemporary styles. An ecclesial identity is constructed through such worship experiences.

As a result of these new emphases and methodologies, youth congregations have become a growing feature of youth evangelism. They may be discrete congregations within existing churches or youth targeted church plants. They may take a cell church approach[5] or be part of an area or deanery strategy. The Church of England's National Youth Office believes that some form of youth congregation now exists within each diocese of the Church of England.

This booklet will attempt to identify and address the conflict between these underlying missiological principles and the current practice in ecclesiology which this issue has revealed, with particular (but not exclusive) reference to the Church of England.

2

Belonging to the Church

My opening theological assumption is that it is not possible to belong to Christ apart from belonging to his church! To be 'in Christ' is to be in his Body. Christianity is necessarily personal but is essentially corporate. Reconciliation with God also implies reconciliation with others. That reconciliation needs to be visibly expressed across racial, cultural and generational barriers. The church is both a community and an institution, and to belong to Christ is to belong to his church in both senses.

Membership of the church is not only a theological necessity, but also a practical one. Faithful discipleship requires actual involvement in the community of Christ because a primary purpose of Christian community is personal and corporate transformation into Christlikeness.[6] 'Christian community is not primarily about togetherness...togetherness happens but only as a by-product of the main project of trying to be faithful to Jesus.'[7] There is clear empirical evidence of a direct relationship between regular church attendance and recognizably Christian behaviour.[8] In other words you *do* have to go to church to live a Christian life!

William Abraham has defined evangelism as 'that set of intentional activities which is governed by the goal of initiating people into the kingdom of God for the first time.'[9] To enter the kingdom requires initial repentance and faith, but its purpose is discipleship. Youth evangelism strategies which do not lead to active participation in the church cannot fulfil the great commission's call to make disciples.[10]

In God's economy there is also an interdependence of worship and mission. The prime calling of the church is Godward in worship, but a life lived for others is also sustained in corporate worship. 'Worship makes strong demands upon us. It requires no less than we should go out into the world to love, serve and care.'[11] The very foundation of Christian witness is a community whose life affirms the plausibility of the gospel. 'People should be able to look at the way we live and begin to understand what the gospel is about. Our life must tell them who Jesus is and what he cares about.'[12] Furthermore, in the postmodern post-Christendom era, 'belonging' to the community of faith will often need to precede 'believing' in that community's gospel.[13]

In theory then, any attempt to win young people to the Christian faith will need to involve 'churching' them. It is when this theory has to be turned into practice that the difficulties increasingly arise. My own perception is that there are greater opportunities to win young people to Christ, and more imaginative youth initiatives, in the UK at present than at any other time in my life.[14] The tragedy is that as evangelism becomes 'easier' there are increasing difficulties in integrating those who respond into the church. As Pete Ward informed the Anglican Evangelical Assembly, 'It's not that young people don't want to become Christians. It's that the church can't handle them when they do.'[15] In part the problem lies in the huge distance between the culture and presuppositions of the church and the majority of young people who have been raised with no knowledge of Christianity whatsoever. We are increasingly dealing with 'pre-Christians' with whom there is practically no common ground of shared religious belief, despite the assumptions of many church people. Sadly, in the words of Bob Mayo, 'The assumption is…that when we talk about "Jesus" people will understand what we are talking about, even if they don't agree…This assumption is wrong.'[16]

From Traditional to Professional

But the difficulty with church is also becoming evident within church-based youth fellowships. Traditional church approaches are losing ground—with most age groups! For example, Sunday attendance at Anglican churches by 14–17 year olds dropped by 34.9% between 1987 and 1996 and that of 18–21 year olds by 34.1%. Church-based youth work that did not require church attendance declined by similar figures.[17] The *English Church Attendance Survey* published in 2000 revealed that 'In the last two decades of the 20th century the number of young people up to 19 in church has halved.'[18] Many effective youth fellowships remain but even they show an increasing dependency on whatever is directly provided by youth leaders, matched by an increasing difficulty in integrating young people into the mainstream worship and programmes of the church. As a result there has been a rapid expansion of youth services and of the employment of youth workers. 'One church in seven held a regular youth worship service…with an average attendance of 43.'[19] One in every five of the churches in the 2000 survey had employed a youth worker.[20] The national Youth Office estimates that the Church of England currently employs through its parishes and initiatives between three and four thousand youth workers. As 'over half the churches in this sample had no young people aged 15 to 18,'[21] this shows a very significant shift towards youth ministry being increasingly led by 'professionals' and involving separate acts of worship. Studies by Springboard have also shown that these services can be a growth factor.[22]

It is this reality that has led to initiatives in developing youth congregations, both to win new young people and to keep those we already have in the fellowship of Christ.

3
The New Context for Youth Mission

In my view this is all evidence that youth ministry is now addressing a 'cultural era' gap, rather than a 'generation' gap.[23] Whatever may be the continuities between modernity and postmodernity (and whatever labels may be chosen if 'post' is not the accepted prefix),[24] there are some substantial discontinuities. This is clearly shown in a recent survey of sociological studies of young people in Britain since the 1970s, which states that 'Young people today are growing up in a different world to that experienced by previous generations.'[25] And that 'The life experience of young people in modern industrialized societies has changed quite significantly over the last two decades.'[26] This social and cultural transition has magnified the tension, always present in youth ministry, that contemporary work with young people will usually make the adult congregation seem 'out of date.' However there *is* an increasingly serious problem about the culture of many churches. 'To become a Christian...you have to find a way of living in a culture that no longer exists in everyday life.'[27] This statement was made in a book, not about youth ministry, but commending some lessons from Willow Creek Community Church for *adult* evangelism in Britain. The culture of the church must not be allowed to impose an additional 'obstacle' to the gospel.[28]

Postmodernity

I have outlined the main features of postmodern culture in a previous booklet.[29] The main co-ordinates are consumerism, electronic networking and globalization. The emphasis is on the construction of identity. David Lyon writes:

'The inflated characteristics of modernity, which give rise to postmodern premonitions, relate above all to communication and information technologies and to the tilt towards consumerism. Both are bound up with the restructuring of capitalism that has been under way since at least the last quarter of the twentieth century.'[30]

In other words, three major transitions interlock and radically change the way we experience and interpret the world. They are the shifts from producer to consumer, from industrial to electronic society and from sovereign nation states to a globalized world.

What I wish to emphasize here is the difference between this culture and the one in which most adult church members were raised. Youth ministry is a cross-cultural mission and it requires new approaches.

Creating identity through lifestyle (consumer) choice is *'novel.'*[31] There has not been a society known to us where this was the everyday practice. 'We have not been here before. We do not know what to expect.'[32] New forms of electronic communication change the way we see and feel the world.

'The growth of communication and information technologies is one of the most striking and transformative changes of the twentieth century. They do not in themselves transform anything, but they contribute to the establishment of *novel* contexts of social interaction...They help to alter the significance of face-to-face relationships while simultaneously bringing all of us into daily contact with cultures once remote or strange.'[33]

And the church has not been good at relating to this new world.

'It is no secret that those most influenced by electronic culture participate in church at far lower levels than those of previous generations. I believe that the failure of the church, as of yet, to deal with the changes brought on by an electronic culture is a basic factor in the lower levels of participation of post-World War 2 electronic generations.'[34]

Once again this is a cultural not merely a generational difference. 'It would be tragic to live through one of the most significant transitions in the history of the world and to relegate it to a mere stage in the life of the young.'[35] The globalized interconnectedness of our world also radically changes the way we experience it. In his Reith lectures Anthony Giddens stated that 'Globalization is *restructuring the ways in which we live*, and in a very profound manner... Globalization also influences everyday life as much as it does events happening on a world scale.'[36]

Most important of all, these social forces change the way we experience time and space.

'The postmodern places question marks over older, modern assumptions about authority, and it foregrounds questions of identity. It does so because at a profound social level, time and space, the very matrix of human social life, are undergoing radical social restructuring.'[37]

We communicate electronically across the world 'in no time.' We live in a society which expects everything to be 'instant.' Distance is no longer an obstacle. So the neighbourhood is no longer a commitment. Mobility is a norm. The power of places to provide identity is being 'replaced' by the power of flows of information, capital and power in a networked society.[38] Whether or not 'postmodern' is the best title for this cultural era, what is clear is that it is both different to what has gone before and 'normal' to young people and young adults. It requires a renewal of imagination about the form of mission and therefore the form of the church.

Post-Christendom

The modern to postmodern transition also coincides with the final demise of Christendom. 'Christendom, as an overarching cohesive body of belief and morals held to by the great majority of the people in the West, is evaporating.'[39] The point is not about theologies of church and state, nor about the rightness of Establishment. It is simply that the attitude of most people to the church—any church—has changed. Church attendance has ceased to be seen as a duty and is increasingly seen as a leisure option.[40] Believing really has been split from belonging. All the major church traditions in this country have been shaped by Christendom—by an expectation that they have a special right to be heard and that people 'ought' to listen to them. Whole strategies of evangelism have been based on a residual guilt about not going to church.[41] But we are now one voice amongst many.[42]

Post-Christendom is not the same as pre-Christendom. A powerful heritage remains. The political world contains many practising Christians. Christendom approaches continue to be effective for the over 60s (among whom the church is growing). But Christendom is now a minority option, a 'lifestyle choice' chosen or assumed by people who are puzzled that others do not choose it, or think of church as they do. But with no more than 7% (perhaps only 4%) of children in any form of 'Sunday School' and with little explicit Christianity taught in most schools, the mainstream church is becoming more and more distanced from the mainstream society. Increasingly it is the case that young people are not so much put off the church as that they do not know what it is!

Stuart Murray urges that in post-Christendom

> 'we have to learn what it means to be a church on the margins rather than at the centre, to operate as a movement rather than an institution, and to become unconventional and surprising rather than predictable.'[43]

In particular, Christendom suggests a stable society shared between church attender and non-attender, and invites a 'come to us' approach to mission. Post-Christendom assumes a cultural divide and requires a 'go-to' contextualized form of church and mission. As Andrew Walls has written,

> 'It is now too late to treat Western society as in some sort of decline from Christian standards, to be brought back to the church by preaching and persuasion. Modern Western society, taken as a whole, reflects one of the great non-Christian cultures of the world.'[44]

4
Pragmatic Missiology

All this implies a significant shift in the focus and ethos of youth ministry. To meet this new situation a pragmatic missiology has taken shape. Despite the fantasies of many church leaders, youth congregations are not a 'bridging strategy.' They are not a temporary way of holding young people in the church 'until they learn to worship properly like the rest of us!' Such a strategy rarely works in other forms of evangelism,[45] and it certainly does not work with today's young people. The youth congregation may well be a young person's only church. The leaders of youth congregations are carrying responsibility for worship, pastoral care, mission and evangelism—and even church planting. Some of the young people *may* also attend a regular service of the parent church, but for many this is their *only* church! It is *not* a bridge to the 'real thing'. It is an experience of the church of Jesus Christ. To treat it as anything less would be to misinterpret its significance and to risk losing many of those who have been genuinely converted.

Within the Church of England the pioneering work of Soul Survivor Watford was set up to be a bridge project, to win young people through regular contact café nights (Dregs Café) and through worship celebrations. The idea was that those won to faith would then be transferred to the home church (St Andrew's, Chorleywood) or to its adult church plant in Watford. Both of these churches had a comparatively contemporary style. If any churches in the area could have been home to them, it would be these. The first part of the strategy worked well, and young people were won for Christ; the second failed totally—they would not go! So the best known youth congregation was, in this sense, an unplanned birth!

Another key example is Eternity youth congregation at Bracknell.[46] The vicar's son returned from university and was given permission to start a Friday night youth worship event. Three years later this congregation is meeting in a school in a neighbouring parish because it is too large for its parent parish church. There are two outreach cafés, a magazine, home groups led by teenagers, and a basketball ministry.

In situations like these, 'congregation' really does mean congregation. It involves worship, a thought-out evangelistic strategy, cell groups with leadership training, a certain amount of experienced pastoral backup, and probably children's work.[47] Above all it involves youth taking actual responsibility for their own ministry.

As effective evangelism all of this is wonderful, but it raises major ecclesiological issues. Can there be any theological basis for a one-generational church? What about authorized leadership and sacramental ministry? What is the relationship between church and locality? What relationship does such a church or congregation have to its parent denomination or to the universal church?

In *The New Testament and the People of God* Tom Wright addresses the problem of the presuppositions with which scholarship tries to recreate Christian origins. His conclusion is that 'The epistemological tools of our age seem inadequate for the data before us.' But his hope is that 'studying Jesus might lead to a reappraisal of the theory of knowledge itself.'[48] There is, I believe, a direct analogy to be drawn regarding ecclesiology. We could say that the ecclesiological practices of our age seem inadequate for the missionary task before us, and that studying youth congregations might lead to a reappraisal of the applied theology of the church itself.

Most of the work with youth congregations is being done by Christians from the evangelical tradition; the cases I have given are also Anglican.

Evangelicals and Ecclesiology

As a cross-denominational movement, evangelicals have never had an agreed basis for ecclesiology beyond their shared commitment to Scripture. Richard Lints has pointed out that Evangelicalism is united around some core doctrines—'Scripture has final authority; God does his saving work in history; eternal salvation is possible only through the atoning death of Christ; we receive salvation only through personal faith in Jesus Christ; evangelism and missions are critically important; it is important to have a spiritually transformed life'.[49] At the same time it lacks a 'common theological tradition.' Lints' list of doctrines prioritizes some dimensions of mission but lacks any reference to ecclesiology. So evangelicals have tended to be missiological pragmatists who derive their ecclesiology from the denomination to which they belong, bending it as and when mission seems to require. In line with this the evangelical tradition in the Church of England has, until recently, tended to be pragmatic rather than theological about ecclesiology. Youth congregations could, then, be dismissed as yet another piece of missiological opportunism which lacks ecclesiological reflection.

The situation has been further complicated by the tendency, pointed out by Pete Ward, for evangelical youth ministry to be missionary in theory but protective in practice.[50] Youth fellowships then become 'safe havens'[51] for the protection of church young people rather than nurturing the dimension of outward-looking mission. A deeper root of this tendency is an understanding of holiness and spiritual protection as 'separation' from the world rather than being Christlike in and for it.[52] Youth congregations, understood as essentially missionary endeavours, offer a way out of this misreading of Scripture.

11

Anglican Ecclesiology

The Anglican 39 Articles define the church as follows: 'The visible church of Christ is a congregation of faithful men, in which the pure word of God is preached, and the sacraments are duly ministered according to Christ's ordinance in all those things that of necessity are requisite to the same.'[53] Despite popular belief, 'Anglicanism does not see the worshipping congregation as the fundamental unit of the church...The Article [XIX] is not primarily referring to what we understand by a worshipping congregation in a parish, but to a national church made up of dioceses. For Anglican ecclesiology the "congregation" in the strict sense is the diocese.'[54] However it may be understood, the article does not raise insuperable theological problems about youth congregations. Under the authority of the bishop such congregations enable young people to join the 'visible' church in a local form. In Anglican terms there are practical questions of authorization: who is authorized to preach and administer the sacraments, and by whom were they authorized? Both at Soul Survivor and at Eternity the bishop has authorized the (lay) congregational leaders and ensured that ordained ministers preside at communion. Soul Survivor Watford now has an ordained Associate Minister. Other congregations are also led by ordained and licensed clergy.

But this is not the end of the Anglican story. Anglican ecclesiology (and Canon Law!) assumes that each 'congregation' is gathered from a particular geographical parish to worship, using authorized liturgies, at the local parish church each Sunday. The article is put into practice with a very specific institutional form. But most youth congregations are not restricted to parish boundaries, their worship is likely to be much looser than authorized liturgies, and their buildings not necessarily consecrated churches. Eternity meets in a school in a neighbouring parish (by consent of the local incumbent, Deanery Synod and Area Bishop) and Soul Survivor meets in an adapted warehouse. So are we to dismiss youth congregations as yet another example of the clash between evangelical pragmatism and denominational structure?

Not so; for it is at this point that imaginative missiological practice reveals the inadequacy of ecclesiological practice. Churches and denominations are vulnerable to the temptation of treating their current practice as the only acceptable way to 'do' church in their tradition. The Lausanne consultation on 'Contextualization Revisited' recognized that 'There are many who still fuse the meaning and forms of the gospel.'[55] In effect we also confuse the meaning and forms of the church, as the fruit of the gospel. The concepts of contextualization or inculturation were developed by the missionary movement.[56] A Christendom mentality could only understand them in relation to mission overseas. But we now know that *all* Christianity is contextualized, *is* not culture-free, nor is it *meant* to be. When context changes church has to change to be faithful to an unchanging gospel.[57] The Church of England is being challenged to re-imagine the way it fulfils its founding article.

The introduction to the Declaration of Assent[58] made by all Church of England clergy at their ordination, and at their installation in any new post, asserts the calling of the church to 'proclaim afresh in each generation' the scriptural and credal faith which it affirms. It is the ecclesiological implications of this commitment which have not always been grasped. 'To proclaim afresh' cannot simply mean saying the same words to a new generation that were said to previous generations, in order to draw them into churches which were shaped by modernity and the closing decades of Christendom. Authentic mission, particularly that which crosses cultures, changes the missionaries. It has ecclesiological implications. In a time of culture change a critical question for any church tradition must be, 'Can you imagine a form of church different from that of your own upbringing or recent experience?' The dying words of a church may well be 'We never did it that way before.'

Mission in a time of cultural transition raises unavoidable questions about the form of the church. This was the case in the New Testament with the issues raised by the Gentile mission. The story of Peter and Cornelius is informative.[59] Peter could not imagine a form of 'church' other than one Jewish in culture. He had no way of separating his cultural upbringing from his interpretation of Scripture. It took an initiative of the Spirit guiding him to a threatening Gentile culture to renew his ecclesiological imagination. The same could happen through initiatives in youth congregations, where Lausanne 'people group' theory, network church plant theory, and experience of churches as targeted congregations is all being applied to youth ministry.

This is not a 'one size fits all' proposal, but an invitation to seek a baptism of the imagination about the form of the church in a changing world. A variety of models for the youth congregation is already in existence. It can be a youth-oriented church plant (Soul Survivor, Watford) or an official youth congregation within a large church (MFI at Holy Trinity Winchester). It can even be a 'church plant' of an existing Youth Congregation placed under the wing of a larger church (Soul Survivor, Harrow), or it can emerge out of detached youth work and come under the wing of a parish (Joy in Oxford). It can be an area celebration (The Mix in Bristol) which may or may not share resources for group leader training. It can be a parish initiative with Deanery support (Eternity, Bracknell). There is some overlap with the 'Alternative Worship' network (Grace at St Mary's Ealing and Joy in Oxford). The types of gathering are quite varied and the ecclesiological vocabulary is used very loosely, but there are still ecclesiological lessons to be learnt. In all probability a youth congregation which will grow into a multigenerational congregation is best developed as a church plant. A youth congregation in an area where all or most young people leave home to go to college is best developed as a targeted congregation within a larger church.

5
Conformed to the World?

Without serious ecclesiological reflection youth congregations could be seen as examples of an inappropriate cultural conformism, reflecting an increasingly fragmented society and a youth culture which is tribal and specializes in temporary alliances. The French sociologist Maffelosi remarks how postmodern

> 'tribal groupings cohere on the basis of their own minor values, and...attract and collide with each other in an endless dance, forming themselves into a constellation whose vague boundaries are perfectly fluid.'[60]

In consumer culture there is a

> 'symbolic gathering around brand-names such as Nike, Apple Macintosh, Nintendo, Calvin Klein and so on, where consumers recognize their tribal status but retain an essentially nomadic existence.'[61]

So is youth church a temporary gathering of essentially nomadic young people who choose for a while to form a tribe around one or other brand name of Christianity? It is certainly the case that

> 'Young people appear to consume the Christian scene in roughly the same way they consume other scenes. That is, they move from one to the other fairly easily and construct their identities from whatever takes their fancy. The exclusivity that characterized both youth culture and the Christian youth culture in the last few decades has largely collapsed.'[62]

It is almost certain that any effective youth congregation will attract people with such assumptions. In fact it has to if it is to reach typical 'unchurched' young people. But the critical point will always be whether these congregations have the ability to persuade the visitors to enter a lifelong pathway of discipleship. There is no reason in principle why this cannot be done, and in the youth congregations which I have observed, it is being done.

But can there be any basis for a one-generational church? Ultimately there cannot. The very idea of 'church' implies the whole called-out people of God and needs to demonstrate the breaking down of the social and cultural barriers which the cross of Christ has made possible. However, this raises many other questions of definition. Does the whole local church have to worship together in one congregation as a norm? If this is the case most parish churches with an early morning communion service, a Parish Eucharist or All Age service, and a remnant still attending Evening Prayer, are following a practice which is theologically unacceptable! In practice the Canons require services of Morning and Evening Prayer and Holy Communion to be said every Sunday without ever implying that all loyal Anglicans will attend three times. Most parishes have at least two congregations and in practice age is one of the factors involved in people's choice of act of worship.[63] So there is more precedent for youth congregations than is at first apparent.

In practice it is the changing cultural and therefore missiological context which has led to the development of youth congregations. Some may well prove to be temporary measures until the wider church develops better habits in welcoming and empowering the young. *But to plant the church in an emerging cultural era has to begin with the young.* Some of these experiments may pioneer ways of being church that will be multigenerational and the mainstream in a few decades time.

Unity and Mission

In discussions about this issue there has been a tendency to let assumptions concerning the unity of the church impede its mission. In the New Testament, when a Jewish church began a Gentile mission, problems about unity were the result of effective mission. The strategy described in 1 Corinthians 9 ('To the Jews I became as a Jew, in order to win Jews...To those outside the law I became as one outside the law so that I might win those outside the law') directly resulted in a new problem of unity between Jew and Gentile. When the initiative was taken to plant local churches in primarily Gentile communities it created the situation in which passages like Romans 9–11, Galatians 3.27f, Ephesians 2.11–22 and Colossians 3.11 had to be written. In other words the question of unity should never be used to prevent evangelistic initiatives. Rather evangelistic initiatives create a new situation where unity has to be worked out on the ground. At this point missiology takes priority over ecclesiology because the gospel creates the church!

Personally I am not comfortable with the expression 'Youth Church', although I recognize that the term church is often used loosely and in a variety of ways.[64] However, I am extremely happy with the view, expressed by Bishop Michael Nazir Ali[65] that 'Youth Congregation' is acceptable as long as the 'parent' church to which it belongs or which planted it no longer refers exclusively to itself as a 'church,' but limits the term for this new local partnership of congregations. The use of terms may be pedantic, but the critical point is that the youth congregation be given equal status as a congregation.

But a discussion of the appropriateness of different terms still does not begin to settle the relationship between missiology and ecclesiology.

6
Missionary Ecclesiology

In recent years there has been a substantial renewal of ecclesiological think-ing. Robin Greenwood has identified the key themes as

> 'a new general awareness of the importance of being deliberately open to the Holy Spirit, the rediscovery of the significance of the trinitarian un-derstanding of God's being, the church as a mirror of God's triune life, the eucharistic centre of the life of the church, the need to be open to the local context, and the importance of the eschatological view of the life of the church.'[66]

These are all applicable to a missionary ecclesiology for youth congrega-tions.

Missio Dei—*The Mission of God*

Both missiology and ecclesiology are rooted in trinitarian theology. We only know that God is Holy Trinity because God is a missionary. The mis-sion which forms the church is the *missio dei*. The church's mission is to share in the mission of God.

> 'Mission has its origin in God. God is a missionary God, a God who crosses frontiers towards the world. In creation God was already the God of mis-sion, with his Word and his Spirit as missionaries. God likewise sent his incarnate Son into the world. And he sent his Spirit at Pentecost. Mission is God giving up himself, his becoming (hu)man, his laying aside of his divine prerogatives and taking our humanity, his moving into the world, in his Son and Spirit.'[67]

'Mission has its origin in the heart of God. God is a fountain of sending love. This is the deepest source of mission. It is impossible to penetrate deeper still: there is mission because God loves people.'[68] So the church is mission-ary by its very nature and both the theory and the practice of ecclesiology must embody that. 'It is not the church that has a mission of salvation to fulfil in the world; it is the mission of the Son and of the Spirit through the Father that includes the church.'[69]

As a consequence the Church of England trains its ordained ministers on the basis that the church is essentially a missionary community, and that they are to be leaders and enablers in the mission of the whole people of God.

> 'The church's task is to serve the mission of God in the world. So, regard-less of the diversity of situations within which it does so, its task is fun-

damentally twofold: to proclaim the creative activity of God by which the world is constituted in its proper nature by God, affirming the world so far as it reflects its proper nature; and to proclaim the redemptive activity of God by which the world is once again given its proper being, thereby to be fulfilled according to God's purposes. In this task it follows, and by its nature seeks to conform to, the work of God—through Jesus Christ and by the Holy Spirit—in and for the world, in order to bring the world to its proper relation to God.'[70]

Mission, then, lies at the heart of the church's being. The church has a missionary ontology. 'There is church because there is mission, not *vice versa*.'[71] Pete Ward has applied this to youth ministry.

'The Christian gospel tells the story of a missionary God...It is this God who calls us and inspires us to reach out to young people. Youth ministry or Christian youth work is therefore grounded in the missionary nature of God. The mission is God's not ours. We are called and inspired by God to participate in his seeking of relationship with all human beings.'[72]

Central to this divine mission is the role of the people of God who are called to share in and reflect the relationships of the persons of the Trinity, and personally embody the purposes of God for creation. What God has achieved in Christ remains to be accomplished now in humanity as a whole, and, through God's redeemed human stewards, in creation at large. It is the work of the Holy Spirit to unite the church to Christ, so that the church's members can together live out a reconciled relationship with God the Father, with each other and with the created world as whole.[73]

This is not just a nice piece of theological theory. It has to be worked out at the local level. 'The local church only has a point when it knowingly commits itself to share in God's mission.'[74] We cannot simply sit back, confident that we know what the Church of England should look like irrespective of our missionary context. It is not declining numbers which are the motivation for new forms of youth mission and church. The numbers are merely a warning sign that we are out of touch with our God-given context. The motivation for new initiatives at being church is found in the power of the gospel itself and in our essential calling to share in the mission of God.

Catholicity

The Church of England understands itself as a national church which has a duty before God to offer the gospel to all and to serve all in Christ's name. That is a core value and it is at the heart of our identity and self-understanding. We have embodied that value in a geographical parochial system as the best means of ensuring our ministry to all. The parochial system embodies a gospel priority—or it used to. The changes in society now mean that people relate increasingly in networks rather than neighbourhoods. 'To live in one place no longer means to live together, and living together no longer means living in the same place.' 'The association of place with community or society is breaking down.'[75] But 'the parochial system is a practice not a value.'[76] It is a practice which only partially fulfils its original value, and as such needs supplementing (not replacing) with additional practices of a network variety and often on a deanery basis. Youth congregations provide a crucial contribution to such a supplement.

From a missiological perspective the question of catholicity is about whom we exclude, wittingly or unwittingly, by our practice of evangelism and forms of church.

> 'The agenda of the local church must always be to include rather than exclude. Unconsciously churches reject large tracts of humanity by failing to make provision for them to find a "space" which they can occupy without automatically denying their culture, music, way of speech, or capacity to handle texts and concepts.'[77]

The form of the church can become a primary means of excluding people from the gospel, or at least from membership of the gospel community. Again, this connects with an understanding of the full scope of the mission of God.

> 'What is mission if not the engagement with God in the entire enterprise of bringing the whole of creation to its intended destiny? A local church cannot claim to be part of this if it fails to work with all ages, if it only serves itself, or if it operates entirely on a Radio 4 model to the exclusion of all else.'[78]

At a time of changing culture, which, I repeat, I believe to be the primary reason for a policy of planting youth congregations, the provision of 'space' for people not like 'us' will often, but not always, require the establishing of a new worshipping community, rather than attempts to change the old. Nor is this necessarily the making of a provision for a minority. The research that preceded the establishing of Soul Survivor, Watford found that only 700 of the 24,000 14 to 24 year olds in the greater Watford area had any contact with any church. Patrick Angier writes:

> 'In the area in which I live and work, over 50% of the town are aged under 35 but about 90% of the churchgoers are aged over 35. A culture-specific congregation planted for under 35s is representative of the majority culture.'[79]

If the church is to be a mirror of God's triune life then it must be marked by self sacrifice, including the sacrifice of much-loved ways of being, and hospitality. 'The Trinity is an open, inviting fellowship, and the Spirit wants the church to be the same.'[80] It can never be an end in itself, and its structures should never be self-serving or self-preserving. Nor can they be frozen in time, for the Church is called to share in the mission of the triune God to restore the whole of creation. It cannot stand still while any part of the created order, and especially any element of the human race—such as the young—is unreached by the saving grace of God.

Eschatology

The church must also be understood eschatologically. As an integral part of the ministry of the Holy Spirit it is called to be an anticipation of the future which God has for the whole world. 'As Christ himself embodied the new humanity as the last Adam, the church also is meant to embody it and anticipate the future of the world.'[81] The church in each location is called to be a sign and foretaste of the new creation. It is to be the community which enjoys and demonstrates God's love and righteousness as a visible reality, in the midst of history. 'The gospel is not a statement about some remote future, it is the dawn of that future in the world.'[82] Inevitably it will be an imperfect anticipation of the future. 'The church in the world will always share in the ambiguities of fallen existence as it waits for the consummation of all things.'[83] But it is called to derive its identity from its future hope. That hope has been secured by the work of Christ in the past. The church has no identity apart from that past, but, *because of that past*, it is essentially forward looking. It is this which makes its engagement with culture so important. It must take shape within a culture so as to point beyond that culture and to be an embodied sign of hope to that culture. Paul teaches that the whole of creation 'waits with eager longing for the revealing of the children of God; for the creation was subjected to futility, not of its own will but by the will of the one who subjected it, in hope that the creation itself will be set free from its bondage to decay and will obtain the freedom of the glory of the children of God.'[84] The church has to be the embodiment of the world's hope in Christ. If it is stuck in a cultural time warp, or only embodied in a previous cultural era, it cannot do that. It will always appear as a conservative force, rather than a force for change and a basis for hope. If it is seen as essentially backward looking it will not be heard when it rightly calls its culture 'back' to the ways of God. Many of today's young people live without long-term hope. They do not even believe modernity's secular hope of 'progress.' Only a church embodied in their emerging culture can be a sign of hope to them.

Christ and the Spirit

The gospel creates the church. Where the gospel is planted church grows.[85] The church grows in its cultural context but also in continuity with what has gone before. There are aspects which are given. It is not the church without them. But it must also adapt to culture. It cannot be the church without that either. In this sense it is shaped by both an internal and an external dynamic.

'A faithful church is continually shaped by its inner dynamic: the flow of apostolic tradition, with Scripture as its norm, in its ministry, teaching, sacraments and outreach. The church is however also shaped by the kind of world in which it finds itself.'[86]

An examination of the distinctive (but interdependent) roles of the Son and the Spirit within the *missio dei* is of particular help here. John Zizioulas has argued that 'Christ in-stitutes (the church) and the Spirit con-stitutes.'[87] Here Christ is the founder of the church and the benchmark against which all forms of church are to be tested, but it is the role of the Spirit, not only to lead people to life in Christ, but to lead the church into appropriate Christ-shaped structures in each particular context. Thus the Spirit is not the possession of the church guaranteeing an unchanging institution, but rather the one who continually re-forms it in Christ. Zizioulas writes: 'The "in-stitution" is something presented to us, more or less a *fait-accompli*...The "con-stitution" is something that involves us in its very being, something that we accept freely because we take part in its very emergence.'[88]

This ecclesiology puts the structural or institutional dimension of the church at the service of its mission, not the other way round. So John Milbank describes the foundational Christian story (metanarrative) as

> 'not just the story of Jesus, it is the continuing story of the church, already realized in a final exemplary way by Christ, yet still to be realized universally, in harmony with Christ, and yet *differently* , by all generations of Christians.'[89]

This statement carefully preserves the final authority of Christ as revealed in Scripture but provides a way of evading the temptation to freeze one form of church structure as though it were the *only* way to be faithful to Christ.

The role of the Spirit as the leader of the church's mission is thus properly acknowledged. 'It is not said that the Spirit will help the disciple to bear witness...What is said is that the Spirit will bear witness and that—secondarily—the disciples are witnesses.'[90] To allow the missionary ontology of the church to shape its form is simply to recognize that 'The Spirit is not the church's auxiliary.'[91] 'The Spirit's role is not a junior role...the church is born and empowered by the Spirit.'[92] This insight in the distinctive roles of the Son and the Spirit in the formation of the church opens up the possibility of Anglican churches developing new forms of church in the course of mission, as a development of their ecclesiology rather than a departure from it. The shape of a missionary church then becomes a matter of the discernment of the Spirit, rather than a one-size-fits-all way of being Anglican. 'The church rides the wind of God's Spirit like a hawk, endlessly and effortlessly circling and gliding in the summer sky. It ever pauses to wait for impulses of power to carry it forward to the nations.'[93]

Incarnation and Contextualization

The incarnation of Christ is not only the final standard by which any embodiment of church must be measured. It is also the foundation of contextual ecclesiology. 'Christ is Word translated.' 'Christianity is culturally infinitely translatable.'[94] The incarnation into a particular culture was for the sake of all cultures. Almost immediately Christianity dispensed with the culture and language of its founder and opened up other languages and cultures. Christianity is pluralist regarding culture. 'Translatability became the characteristic mode of Christian expansion through history.'[95] Ecclesiology is contextual because Christianity is founded on the incarnation.

It will not do to sit outside this culture and try to communicate into it. We have to be willing to immerse ourselves in it. As David Lyon says, 'Religious life in postmodern times demands not only to be understood differently, but also to be lived differently.'[96] What is needed is an incarnational approach to culture and therefore to the form of the church. Tex Sample makes this challenge:

> 'The issue is not relevance as far as the church is concerned. The issue is incarnation. When so-called "traditional" churches are out of touch with the people who live around them, the problem is not that they are irrelevant, but that they are not incarnational.'[97]

He rightly points out the need to be counter-cultural, particularly to consumerism as an ideology[98]—but counter-cultural from the inside, not from the outside. God in Christ entered our context. Christian mission requires us to do the same. Faithfulness to Christ combines incarnation with costly obedience.

> 'The call here is for a church that will "imitate" Christ, to pitch tent, to embody itself, to take form in the indigenous practices of our time, not for the purpose of accommodation, but to be God's people. It is a twofold effort: To join the practices of an electronic culture, on the one hand, and to keep faith with the story of Christ, on the other.'[99]

'Communion'

In recent years the renewal of trinitarian theology has enabled a remarkable ecumenical renewal of ecclesiology, particularly around the theme of 'communion.'[100]

The second helpful contribution from trinitarian theology is that of 'perichoresis,' the mutuality of the persons of the Trinity. The simplest explanation of this technical term is given by Robin Greenwood:

> 'The three Persons of the Trinity in perichoretic relationship do not simply take up an attitude of loving concern towards each other, but actually make each other who they are through living relation. Their separate but

different contribution to the trinitarian being and work is inseparable from the relationship between them.'[101]

When applied to the church this gives primacy to mutual relationship and recognition, and makes that the context and moderating influence on hierarchy, tradition and the exercise of authority. This would enable the sort of inter-congregational recognition and mutuality suggested by Michael Nazir Ali above. It allows difference and interdependence. New forms of congregation may be planted, whether as youth mission or any other, but a relationship of interdependence is maintained with the original church. Each gives identity to the other. The youth congregation could not exist apart from the resourcing of its 'parent,' but the founding congregation is no longer the same. Like a couple having a first child, a new dimension has entered its life.

Clearly then, formal relations with parent churches and with denominations are theologically and not just functionally important if youth congregations are to be authentic expressions of the church of Christ. Youth congregations need to be in relationships where they are owned, not just left to sink or swim, and where they are answerable to proper authority at parochial and diocesan level. It will also be important that they develop recognized and authorized forms of ministry if they are to have any ongoing relationship with other churches!

Eucharist

Robin Greenwood's list of key themes in the renewal of ecclesiological thinking included 'the eucharistic centre of the life of the church.' Theologically, I agree. Holy Communion is the central act of Christian worship and the place where the church renews its sense of identity, its inheritance from the past and its true basis for hope. 'Christ has died, Christ is risen, Christ will come again.' As such it needs to lie at the heart of any long term youth congregation. Pete Ward has argued for 'a contextualization of Communion within contemporary culture that remains connected to the residue of gospel truth seen in the tradition of the church.'[102] He also argues for the counter-cultural power of the eucharist within youth cultures. The eucharist is indeed powerful refocusing on the gospel's three-dimensional hope in a largely one-dimensional consumer society.[103] This does not mean that every service in a youth congregation should be Communion. I believe the Church of England's wholesale buying into the Parish Communion movement has robbed us of missionary flexibility and made our regular services excluding of the enquirer. In a culture where belonging precedes believing we have to be very careful about the barriers we raise. Nevertheless, eucharistic provision must be at the heart of the Church of England's owning of its youth congregations.

7
A Baptism of Imagination

If the church is essentially missionary, and if Anglican theologians and official Anglican documents are saying so, why the tension between missiology and ecclesiology? In his commentary on Article XIX, Professor Oliver O'Donovan wrote that

> 'there has to be a bridge between evangelical theology and ecclesiastical theory; that is, there has to be a theology of the church as such, which in turn will be the basis for the administrative tasks of church organization. That theology must not detract from the place of Christ at the centre of the gospel message.'[104]

It seems to be the case that a particular form of Anglican ecclesiological organization is, in some circumstances, in increasing tension with the ontology of the church, its trinitarian and missionary nature. There is thus an urgent need for the ontology to be allowed to shape the ecclesiological structures. Serious trinitarian reflection on the nature and missiological necessity of youth congregations gives the Church of England the opportunity to do this.

My research has been limited to Anglican youth congregations and area celebrations with Anglican involvement. There are contacts with New Church experiments and one early congregation was lost to the New Churches because the Church of England could not provide it with a home. It would be *an avoidable tragedy* if this were to happen again, as a number of good ecclesiological models are available. Genuine church plants can operate according to the guidelines in the House of Bishops' report *Breaking New Ground.* Where the plant is in a different parish or deanery from its parent, the local incumbent can act as chaplain (Soul Survivor, Watford). The congregational leader can be commissioned by the bishop (Eternity). Youth congregations can be treated as deanery ventures or have deanery support (Eternity). They can be directly answerable to the Bishop via his Diocesan Youth Officer (an earlier Blackburn pattern for Alternative Worship Groups). They can report regularly to the bishop (Warehouse, York) or even be set up at the invitation of the bishop (Soul Survivor, Harrow and Ignite, Willesden Episcopal Area). Confirmation services provide a vital link with episcopal ministry. In all the cases I have explored, sacramental ministry (baptisms and Holy Communion) is carried out by whatever clergy are recognized as having official oversight (vicar or chaplain). Many of the more recent experiments with youth congregations have been on a deanery basis as the deanery becomes a strategic missionary unit and clergy learn to work more collaboratively and be less defensive of their territory. 'The parish system with its many buildings must now be secondary to the redevelopment of the idea of the local church as a locally negotiated area of collaborative ministry.'[105]

Anglican youth congregations will also need to develop appropriate patterns of Anglican family likeness which are culturally appropriate to the young people they are trying to reach. In this way they will be able to pioneer new forms of Anglicanism for a changing culture. It is particularly critical that the appropriate use of liturgy is thought through. *Common Worship* provides much more flexible resources as a starting point. The musical ability in several youth congregations is such that sung liturgy within their usual musical genre could easily be developed.

We are in practice seeing the emergence of new forms of church within the Church of England. The Holy Spirit is baptizing our imaginations about the form of the church. Youth congregations are only one example—but they are a pressing one. 'It is still true that over 70% of those who come to faith do so before the age of 20. It is older teenagers being converted in the 1990s whereas it was younger teenagers in the 1980s.'[106]

<hr>

8
The Joy and the Pain

It has to be admitted that these developments can be an agony for many older church members and older congregations. They rightly ask 'how will our young people learn the tradition?' The reality is that many will not learn the tradition as older Anglicans know it. (Some will; I am not suggesting that traditional church for young people is dead, simply that it is not enough.) It takes courage to release young people for something new.

The church's work among young people combines continuity with change. It *begins* with its responsibility to pass on its faith to the next generation (1 Cor 15.1–4, 2 Tim 2.2). It *continues* with the responsibility to be open to change, as it listens to the Spirit of Christ in the young. Without this openness to listen, Christian mission can be trapped in a time warp and become ineffective.

In all probability many of our current forms and ways of being church will not prove adequate in the emerging society. It is young people whom we help to faith and equip to shape the emerging culture who will also need to develop new forms of worship and church structure which will one day be the mainstream.

It is unrealistic and inappropriate to expect the majority of congregations to adapt to an emerging culture in which they have not been nurtured. Crucial to the church's mission will be the ability to recognize, release and support young adult leaders who are at ease in the new developments. We need to take the risk of trusting such leaders with responsibility to experiment with new forms of worship and discipleship. The theological foundation of such trust is found in the 'eschatological' Holy Spirit whose role is to bring the foretaste of God's future into the present. When the practices of the past are of limited usefulness, it is the work of the Holy Spirit in the next generation of leaders which we must trust. Have we the courage and grace to do so?[107]

My conclusion is that the questions raised by youth congregations provide a significant learning point for the Church of England just as it is seeking to be more of a missionary church. Anglican theologians are re-imagining the practice of ministry in the light of the Trinity. Anglican ordinands are being trained as those who lead the people of God as it shares in the *missio dei*. Anglican foundational documents do not inhibit these developments. Recent Anglican reports provide key encouragement or precedent. The report *Eucharistic Presidency* locates its understanding of the Church in the doctrine of the Trinity.[108] The report *Working As One Body* sees 'The bishop with his diocese as the pivotal unit of the church.'[109] This allows for cross-parish or deanery-based youth initiatives. The report *Breaking New Ground* allows for network, not just neighbourhood church plants.[110] The report *Youth A Part* identifies youth work as participation in the *missio dei* which involves the crossing of cultural barriers.[111]

What is needed is not so much a change of structures as a new imagination in the way we use them.[112] Youth congregations may or may not prove to be an ongoing feature of the Church of England, but they can belong to the Church of England without being made to feel alien; and they can help the Church of England to discover the shape of its future. It only requires missiology to be allowed to reshape ecclesiology.

Notes

1 Timothy Yates, *Christian Mission in the Twentieth Century* (CUP, 1994) p 127.
2 Peter Brierley, *Christian England* (Marc Europe, 1991).
3 'The decline in older teens and those in their 20s is more in line with population movements.' 'The 15 to 19 age-group is the only one (apart from 65 and over) where the loss is less in the 1990s than the 1980s.' Peter Brierley, *The Tide Is Running Out* (Christian Research, 2000) pp 97–8.
4 As exemplified by the Message to Schools 'Eden Projects' in Greater Manchester
5 See 'Youth Cells at St Alkmund's Derby' in *Cell Church Stories as Signs of Mission* (Grove Evangelism booklet Ev 51).
6 Ephesians 4.13.
7 Stanley Hauerwas and William Willimon, *Resident Aliens* (Abingdon, 1989) p 78.
8 See William Kay and Leslie Francis, *Drift From the Churches* (University of Wales, 1996), Robin Gill, *Churchgoing and Christian Ethics* (CUP, 1999).
9 William Abraham, *The Logic of Evangelism* (Eerdmans, 1989) p 95.
10 Matthew 28.16–20.
11 Robin Gill, *Moral Communities* (University of Exeter, 1992) p 23.
12 Jim Wallis, *Call to Conversion* (Lion, 1986) p 108.
13 See Grace Davie, *Religion in Britain Since 1945—Believing Without Belonging* (Blackwell, 1994).
14 Among the developments I have in mind are youth congregations, youth cells, night-club chaplaincies, schools initiatives and a rich experimentation in worship.
15 Pete Ward addressing the Anglican Evangelical Assembly, May 1995.
16 Bob Mayo 'Evangelism Among pre-Christian Young People' p 71 in *Relational Youthwork*, Pete Ward (ed) (Lynx, 1995).
17 *Youth A Part* (Church House Press, 1996) p 13.
18 Peter Brierley, *The Tide Is Running Out*, p 95.
19 *ibid*, p 162.
20 *ibid*, p 168.
21 *ibid*, p 169.
22 Robert Warren and Bob Jackson, 'There Are Answers' (Springboard Resource Paper 1).
23 See my chapter (2) in *Youth A Part*, sections 2.9–2.14.
24 See *Postmodernity*, David Lyon (Open University Press, 1994); *Telling the Story*, Andrew Walker (SPCK, 1996); *Liquid Modernity*, Zygmunt Bauman (Polity, 2000).
25 Andy Furlong and Fred Cartmel, *Young People and Social Change* (Open University, 1997) p 5.
26 *ibid*, p 1.
27 Martin Robinson, *A World Apart* (CPAS/Monarch, 1992) p 37.
28 1 Cor 9.13.
29 *Postmodern Culture and Youth Discipleship* (Grove Pastoral booklet P 76).
30 David Lyon, *op cit*, p 7.
31 Anthony Giddens, *Modernity and Self Identity* (Polity 1991) p 199.
32 Zygmunt Bauman with Keith Tester, *Conversations With Zygmunt Bauman* (Polity, 2001) p 128.
33 David Lyon, *Jesus in Disneyland*, p 13.
34 Tex Sample, *op cit*, p 15.
35 Tex Sample, *op cit*, p 16.
36 Anthony Giddens, *Runaway World* (Profile, 1999) p 4.

37 David Lyon, *ibid*, p 11.

38 Manuel Castells, *The Rise of the Network Society* (Blackwell, 2nd ed, 2000).

39 John Finney, *Recovering the Past* (DLT, 1996) p 1.

40 Grace Davie, *Religion in Britain Since 1945* (Blackwell, 1994) p 194.

41 As with the initial growth of Willow Creek Community Church with its Seeker services.

42 For an overview of these changes see Eddie Gibbs and David Coffey, *Church Next* (IVP, 2001) ch 1.

43 Stuart Murray 'A Decade of Experimentation—Redesigning Church for Post-Christen-dom' in *The Bible in Transmission* (Bible Society, Summer 2001). Stuart Murray writes from an Anabaptist viewpoint. See also his *Church Planting* (Paternoster Press, 1998) chs 5 and 6, and his Grove Evangelism booklet *Hope from the Margins* (Ev 49).

44 Andrew Walls 'Western Society Presents a Missionary Challenge' in *Missiological Education for the 21st Century,* Dudley Woodbury (ed) (Orbis, 1996) p 19.

45 'All Age' services often grow a new congregation; they are rarely effective as transit camps into a more traditional service.

46 'Eternity—the beginning,' *Encounters on the Edge No 4* (Church Army, Sheffield Centre).

47 Two teenage single mothers were among the first young people led to Christ through Soul Survivor, Watford.

48 N T Wright, *The New Testament and the People of God* (SPCK, 1992) p 96.

49 Richard Lints, *The Fabric of Theology* (Eerdmans, 1993) p 49ff.

50 Pete Ward, *Growing Up Evangelical* (SPCK, 1996) ch 7.

51 *ibid*, p 166.

52 See Mike Riddell, *Threshold of the Future* (SPCK, 1998) ch 5.

53 Article XIX.

54 Paul Avis, *An Anglican Understanding of the Church* (SPCK, 2000) p 77.

55 Initial report on 'Contextualization Revisited' (Haslev, Denmark, 1997).

56 See David Bosch, *Transforming Mission* (Orbis 1991) pp 420–432, 447–455

57 See 1 Cor 9.19–23 'I do it all for the sake of the gospel.'

58 *Alternative Service Book 1980*, p 387f, paragraph 12.

59 See *Threshold of the Future*, Mike Riddell (SPCK, 1998) (I have many points of detail and some of substance where I differ from Riddell, but his use of the Cornelius narrative is still instructive).

60 Michel Maffelosi quoted in Chris Rojek, *Decentring Leisure* (Sage, 1995) p 151.

61 Chris Rojek, *Decentring Leisure* (Sage, 1995) p 151f.

62 Pete Ward, *Mass Culture* (BRF, 1999) p 26.

63 Early morning *Book of Common Prayer* communion services, and (bizarrely!) 'All Age' services are two examples.

64 See Pete Ward, *Youth Work and the Mission of God* (SPCK, 1997) ch 7.

65 In answer to a question after a lecture to the Cambridge Theological Federation.

66 Robin Greenwood, *Practising Community* (SPCK, 1996) p 25.

67 David Bosch, *Witness to the World* (Marshalls, 1980) p 239.

68 David Bosch, *Transforming Mission*, (Orbis, 1991) p 392.

69 Jurgen Moltmann, *The Church in the Power of the Holy Spirit*, p 64.

70 ACCM Occasional Paper 22, pp 27–28. This is the document which all ordination training institutions had to respond to each five years for the accreditation of their courses.

71 David Bosch, *Transforming Mission* (Orbis, 1991) p 390.

72 Pete Ward, *Youthwork and the Mission of God* (SPCK, 1997) pp 25–26.

73 For much of the following section I am indebted to my colleague the Rev'd Dr Jeremy Begbie. See in particular the House of Bishops report 'Eucharistic Presidency' which he drafted (notably for this issue chapter 2).

74 Robin Greenwood, *ibid*, p 33.

75 Ulrich Beck, *What Is Globalization?* (Polity, 2000) p 74.
76 Rt Rev'd Mike Hill at the National Anglican Church Planting Conference.
77 Greenwood, *ibid*, p 27f.
78 Greenwood, *ibid*, p 28.
79 Patrick Angier, *Changing Youth Worship* (CHP, 1997) p 64.
80 Clark Pinnock, *Flame of Love* (Downers Grove: IVP, 1996) p 117.
81 Pinnock, *ibid*, p 117.
82 Jurgen Moltmann, *The Church in the Power of the Spirit* (SCM, 1977) p 77.
83 Kevin Giles, *What On Earth Is the Church?* (SPCK, 1995) p 195.
84 Romans 8.19–21.
85 1 Cor 3.5–9.
86 Rt Rev'd Michael Nazir Ali, 'Shapes of the Church to Come.' Discussion paper for the House of Bishops. See also his book of the same name (Kingsway, 2001).
87 John Zizoulos, *Being As Communion* (St Vladimir's Press, 1993) p 140, also referred to by Colin Gunton in *The Forgotten Trinity*, Vol III (London: BCC, 1989) p 128.
88 John Zizoulos, *Being As Communion* (St Vladimir's Press, 1993) p 140.
89 John Milbank, *Theology and Social Theory* (Blackwell, 1990) p 387.
90 Lesslie Newbigin, *The Light Has Come* (SPCK, 1982) p 207
91 *ibid*, p 208.
92 Pinnock, *op cit*, p 115.
93 Pinnock, *op cit*, p 114.
94 Andrew Walls, *The Missionary Movement in Christian History* (T&T Clark, 1996) p 25.
95 Lamin Sanneh, *Translating the Message* (Orbis, 1993) p 214.
96 David Lyon, *ibid*, p 144.
97 Tex Sample, *The Spectacle of Worship in a Wired World* (Abingdon, 1998) p 105.
98 Tex Sample, *ibid*, p 121f.
99 Tex sample, *ibid*, p 122.
100 An excellent Anglican engagement with this is *Transforming Priesthood* by Robin Greenwood (SPCK, 1994). See also Miroslav Volf, *After Our Likeness* (Eerdmans, 1998) for a dialogue between Free Church, Orthodox and Roman Catholic ecclesiologies.
101 Robin Greenwood, *Practising Community* (SPCK, 1996) p 47.
102 Pete Ward (ed), *Mass Culture* (BRF, 1999) p 13.
103 See my chapter 'The eucharist and the postmodern world' in Ward, *ibid*.
104 Oliver O'Donovan, *On the Thirty Nine Articles* (Paternoster Press, 1986) p 93.
105 Greenwood, *ibid*, p 26.
106 Peter Brierley, *The Tide Is Running Out*, p 170.
107 These paragraphs are from my theology chapter in *Youth A Part* (ch 2).
108 *Eucharistic Presidency* (Church House Publishing, 1997).
109 *Working As One Body* (Church House Publishing, 1995).
110 *Breaking New Ground* (Church House Publishing, 1994). See also *Youth A Part*, 4.11–4.12
111 *Youth A Part*, ch 2. See also Pete Ward, *Youth Work and the Mission of God* (SPCK, 1997) ch 2.
112 The precedent is now established of recognizing new work church plants as 'extra-parochial places' under the Pastoral Measure.